The Myth of Water

PRAISE FOR *The Myth of Water*

"Jeanie Thompson's highly tactile *The Myth of Water* is woven like burlap cloth with a warp of prose narrative and a woof of poetry that miraculously make Helen Keller's emotional life and intellectual process palpable for readers. Thompson's poetic technique depends on metaphor—on what is like what—on kinship and the surprise of recognition. This approach is the reverse of 'normal' poetry-making and 'normal' learning, when we hear and see directly *what is*, and *then* it takes flight in metaphor and abstraction. Through Thompson's inspired and inspiring poetry, we experience Helen Keller's world from the inside to the contiguous world. These poems, of world significance, will break your heart, then mend it and return it to you enlarged. The brilliance of these poems makes me weep with joy."

—SENA JETER NASLUND, author of *Ahab's Wife: or, The Star-Gazer; Abundance: A Novel of Marie Antoinette*; and *The Fountain of St. James Court: or, Portrait of the Artist as an Old Woman*

"In *The Myth of Water* Jeanie Thompson, through Helen Keller's persona, moves us beyond the five sensory dimensions we've come to privilege. Here are the sixth, seventh, and eighth senses, the unseen. These are the ones connecting us with the larger unseen and unheard universe. Why watch and hear water when you can be water: 'I was alone,/ tumbling/ in the deep element of myself.' Thompson's world is indeed deep and at times unnerving. Although we know how this story ends, the thoughtful syntax and unexpected images anchors us in an immediate now experience. This is not historical poetry, this is a commentary on the myth of limitation."

—DERRICK HARRIELL, author of *Ropes* and *Stripper in Wonderland*

"Jeanie Thompson, through an act of sympathetic imagination, enters the Helen Keller story, relives it from the inside, and presents it here to readers, fresh, reimagined and, yes, a miracle. If we thought there was nothing new to be said or learned about Helen Keller, Jeanie Thompson's new book shows us how wrong we would be to think that. *The Myth of Water* is a revelation."

—RICHARD TILLINGHAST, author of *Wayfaring Stranger* and *The Stonecutter's Hand*

"This is a moving and wholly satisfying collection of poetry. This collection is satisfying as a work of poetry, a work of biography, and a work of spiritual contemplation."

—MAURICE MANNING, author of *The Common Man* and *Lawrence Booth's Book of Visions*

"While it is hard to find a contemporary poet able to conjure any human figure, much less one so sealed in stone as Helen Keller, in Thompson's *The Myth of Water* Helen lives. She is present. Had I not read these simple poems I would not have believed they could have been written."

—LOUIE SKIPPER, author of *The Work Ethic of the Common Fly* and *It Was the Orange Persimmon of the Sun*

"In *The Myth of Water*, Jeanie Thompson investigates the life of Helen Keller through an aesthetic imagination drawing on memory, culture and the historical to give us this seminal text. These poems are meticulous, lyrical, edifying. Midway through this collection the reader will begin to see the world through Keller's eyes, not the darkness but the everlasting light."

—RANDALL HORTON, author of *Hook: A Memoir*

Helen Keller, No. 9.

The Myth of Water

Poems from the Life of Helen Keller

JEANIE THOMPSON

The University of Alabama Press ❧ Tuscaloosa

The University of Alabama Press
Tuscaloosa, Alabama 35487-0380
uapress.ua.edu

Inquiries about reproducing material from this work should be addressed to
the University of Alabama Press.

Typeface: Garamond Premiere Pro

Cover image: *Hands* by Wayne Sides
Cover and interior design: Michele Myatt Quinn

Library of Congress Cataloging-in-Publication Data
Names: Thompson, Jeanie, author.
Title: The myth of water : poems from the life of Helen Keller /
Jeanie Thompson.
Description: Tuscaloosa, Alabama : University of Alabama Press, [2016]
Identifiers: LCCN 2015049820 | ISBN 9780817358570 (paperback) |
ISBN 9780817389925 (e-book)
Subjects: | BISAC: POETRY / American / General.
Classification: LCC PS3570.H6254 A6 2016 | DDC 811/.54—dc23
LC record available at http://lccn.loc.gov/2015049820

Also by Jeanie Thompson

POETRY

Lotus and Psalm (chapbook)

How to Enter the River

Litany for a Vanishing Landscape (with photos by Wayne Sides)

Ascent (chapbook)

Witness: Poems

White for Harvest: New and Selected Poems

The Seasons Bear Us

PROSE

The Remembered Gate: Memoirs by Alabama Writers,

edited with Jay Lamar

In Memory of Katherine Wade Thompson

(1927–2015)

Contents

PROLOGUE

I

YOU ARE HELEN: 1880–1917

II

BRIDGE: HELEN KELLER'S JOURNAL, 1936–1937

III

YOUR LIGHT: 1943–1948

IV

COMING THROUGH FIRE: CIRCA 1955

V

TELL THE WORLD: 1950–PRESENT DAY

CODA

Writing about Helen Keller

Born in Tuscumbia, Alabama, in 1880, Helen Keller became an international citizen who conquered her disabilities of blindness and deafness brought on by a sudden illness at age nineteen months. Taught by Anne Sullivan Macy, who also suffered semi-blindness, Keller surged ahead through educational experiences that included a bachelor of arts from Radcliff (cum laude) and later an honorary degree from Harvard University, the first presented to a woman. In her eighty-eight years, she visited thirty-five countries on five continents and met with world leaders, sharing her concern for disabled citizens in their countries, especially women and children.

Keller gave her empathy and hope to cultures across a stunning lifetime. In addition, she was an advocate for equity for the deaf-blind in work and society, a suffragist for women's right to vote, and a sympathizer with the American labor movement in the 1930s. She visited Japan before and after the devastating nuclear bombs. Keller experienced firsthand, without major hindrance from her double disability, world history unfolding around her as few have. A woman whose heart opened naturally and passionately to love, she experienced personal heart-break and profound grief, and found avenues through which to serve and expand that love to the entire world.

Keller chose her very public life as much as it chose her. She did not *overcome* her disability as a deaf-blind woman; she *came through it*, gathering her abilities to achieve a meaningful life. For Keller, taking on the world was a "daring adventure, or nothing at all." Long before she died

Keller had become an icon of the world. Her presence became synonymous with sacred wisdom and concern. What is often forgotten is the inevitable tragedy that was at the heart of the miracle of communication and self-discovery that was hers as a child in Alabama in a story we think of as common knowledge.

It is hard to imagine anyone not putting Anne Sullivan, later Macy, in the pantheon of teachers. Yet, we might well mislead ourselves to think of her as we might a favorite teacher, somebody to remember pleasantly when she occasionally comes to mind. Sullivan gave to Keller the capacity for self-understanding and the literal art of configuring the world that made Keller into a secular saint. Giving Keller the key to a fully expressed life and a profound love of literature, Sullivan became an essential part of her pupil, as all profound teachers are. Keller was fifty-six years old when Sullivan, virtually blind herself, died. As much as Keller's was a lifetime of giving, hers was a life of mourning her teacher's absence as she worked for the rights of disabled people everywhere to live, work, and love as all other human beings.

These poems struggle with the humanity behind the name *Helen Keller*. Choosing to write historical persona poems because they seemed the best vehicle to dramatically portray the person I perceived Keller to be, I sought to reveal a woman less known than the famous world citizen the public adored. Poetry takes many approaches, and as such these poems are based in documented fact filtered through distillations of readings and impressions. Some are fantasias of how Keller might have felt or thought, or how she responded as a woman in a particular circumstance.

It is my hope that these poems give a sense of Keller's simple humanity and great heart. If they work at all, they will bring more people to appreciate Helen Keller, a woman who sought justice above all else.

Important Texts

These poems are based on facts of Helen Keller's life but should be considered a work of the imagination, even fiction at times, depicting the life of an extraordinary woman.

I am indebted to the biography *Helen Keller: A Life* by Dorothy Hermann, and to Keller's *A Light in My Darkness*, both of which led me to the expression of her spiritual life and her attendant artistic sensibility. *The World I Live In, Midstream, Teacher, Helen Keller's Journal,* and other writings of Keller's gave me the window into her world I needed to imagine her as a private woman driven to public service, sometimes at the expense of her own emotional life.

I was further inspired by the fact that Helen Keller was born in North Alabama and spent her early life there, as I did. She also experienced a turning point at her sister's home on Felder Avenue, a few blocks from where I was living in Montgomery, Alabama, when I learned more of her life story. The scholar Kim E. Nielsen validated my belief in the project when I heard her say on the DVD *Shining Soul: Helen Keller's Spiritual Life and Legacy* that there was a Keller yet to know. And of course Dorothy Hermann concurs in her introduction when she poses the simple question, "Who was Helen Keller?" To these major sources I am grateful and offer thanks.

In addition to those previously mentioned, *Helen Keller: Selected Writings*, edited by Kim E. Nielsen, was particularly useful in guiding me through the enormous body of Keller's books, essays, letters, and other writings. Joseph Lash's encyclopedic *Helen and Teacher* and the revised, expanded edition of Helen's landmark autobiography, *The Story of My Life*, edited by Dorothy Hermann and Roger Shattuck, provided the grounding data of Helen Keller's life and achievement. I am deeply grateful to the work of the staff at The American Foundation for the Blind on whose web site, www.afb.org, I viewed numerous photographs, recordings, and other resources. A variety of works have been consulted in the research of this project.

The timeline included here is from *To Love This Life: Quotations by Helen Keller*, copyright © AFB Press, American Foundation for the Blind, accessed on www.afb.org.

Chronology of Helen Keller's Life

June 27, 1880   Helen Keller is born to Captain Arthur Henley Keller and Kate Adams Keller at Ivy Green in Tuscumbia, Alabama.

February 1882   After being struck by illness, Helen loses both her sight and hearing. No definitive diagnosis of the disease is ever determined.

Summer 1886   The Keller family meets with Dr. Alexander Graham Bell, who recommends contacting Michael Anagnos, director of Perkins Institution for the Blind in Boston. Captain Keller writes to Anagnos, requesting a teacher for Helen. Anagnos contacts his star pupil and valedictorian, Anne Mansfield Sullivan.

March 3, 1887   Anne Sullivan arrives in Tuscumbia and begins teaching Helen manual sign language.

April 5, 1887   Anne makes the "miracle" breakthrough, teaching Helen that "everything had a name," by spelling W-A-T-E-R into Helen's hand as water from the family's water pump flows over their hands.

May 1888– October 1894	Anne, Helen, and Kate Keller travel north, visiting Alexander Graham Bell, and meeting President Grover Cleveland at the White House, and visiting Anagnos at Perkins Institution. Helen continues her education at the Perkins Institute, then the Wright-Humanson School for the Deaf in New York City.
August 19, 1896	Helen's father, Captain Keller, dies. That fall she becomes a devout Swedenborgian.
October 1896	Helen is accepted as a pupil at the Cambridge School for Young Ladies, in preparation for attendance at Harvard's annex for women, Radcliffe College.
December 1897	Helen and Anne leave the Cambridge School and move to Wrentham, Massachusetts. Helen continues her college preparatory studies with the assistance of private tutors.
September 1900	Helen becomes a member of the freshman class of 1904 at Radcliffe.
March 1903	With the help of editor John Albert Macy, Helen writes *The Story of My Life*.
Spring 1904	Helen and Anne buy a home on seven acres of land in Wrentham.
June 28, 1904	Helen becomes the first deaf-blind individual to receive a bachelor of arts degree, graduating cum laude from Radcliffe.
May 3, 1905	Anne marries John Macy at Wrentham.
July 1908	Helen writes and publishes *The World I Live In*.

Spring, 1909   Helen and John Macy join the Socialist Party of Massachusetts, and Helen becomes a suffragist.

January 1913   Helen and Anne begin their career on the lecture circuit. Helen writes and publishes *Out of the Dark*, a collection of socialist writings.

1914   John Macy leaves Anne, though they never officially divorce, and Polly Thomson joins Helen and Anne's household.

November 1916   Peter Fagan, John Macy's assistant, proposes to Helen, and they take out a marriage license in Boston. Helen's mother forces her to publicly renounce her engagement. Helen is sent to Montgomery, Alabama, to visit family, while Anne and Polly travel to Lake Placid and Puerto Rico in hopes of aiding Anne's failing health. While in Montgomery, Helen and Peter plan to elope, according to many sources, but he doesn't arrive at the appointed time to take her away.

October 1917   Helen and Anne sell their farm in Wrentham and move with Polly to Forest Hills, New York.

May 1918   *Deliverance*, a silent film based on Helen's life, is produced.

February 1920   Helen and Anne begin their vaudeville career.

June 1921   Helen's mother, Kate Keller, dies.

October 1924   Helen and Anne begin their work with the American Foundation for the Blind.

June 1925	Helen makes an appeal before the International Convention of Lions Clubs, asking the Lions to become "Knights of the Blind."
October 1927	*My Religion*, Helen's account of her Swedenborgian beliefs, is published.
Spring 1929	*Midstream*, an autobiographical account of Helen's later life, is published.
April 1930	Helen, Anne, and Polly travel abroad for the first time, visiting Scotland, Ireland, and England for over six months.
April 1931	Helen, Anne, and Polly participate in the first World Council for the Blind.
August 1931	Helen, Anne, and Polly travel to France and Yugoslavia.
August 26, 1932	John Macy dies in Pennsylvania.
December 1932	Helen is elected to AFB's board of trustees.
June 1933	Helen, Anne, and Polly return to Scotland.
October 20, 1936	Anne Sullivan Macy dies.
November 1936– January 1937	Helen and Polly travel abroad, visiting England, Scotland, and France.
April 1937	Helen and Polly travel to Japan, Korea, and Manchuria.
Spring 1938	*Helen Keller's Journal*, a personal account of Helen's life in 1936 and 1937, is published.
September 1939	Helen sells her home in Forest Hills, and the household moves to Arcan Ridge in Westport, Connecticut.

January 1943	Helen begins her visits to the blinded, deaf, and disabled soldiers of World War II in military hospitals around the country. She calls this "the crowning experience of my life."
October 1946	Helen and Polly make their first world tour for the American Foundation for the Overseas Blind (AFOB), AFB's sister organization, visiting London, Paris, Italy, Greece, and Scotland. In the next 11 years, they would visit 35 countries on five continents.
November 1946	A fire destroys Arcan Ridge, along with almost all of the household's possessions.
September 1947	The household moves into Arcan Ridge 2, an almost identical replica of the original Arcan Ridge home.
April–August 1948	Helen and Polly begin a tour of Australia and New Zealand as representatives of the AFOB. When they reach Japan, Polly suffers her first stroke, and the remainder of the tour is canceled.
Spring 1950– Spring 1953	Helen and Polly continue to travel all over the world, including Europe, South Africa, the Middle East, and Latin America.
Winter 1953	A documentary film of Helen's life, *The Unconquered* (later renamed *Helen Keller in Her Story*), is released. The film wins an Academy Award for best feature length documentary of 1955.
February 1955	Helen and Polly embark on a tour of the Far East, including India and Japan.

June 1955	Helen receives an honorary degree from Harvard University, the first woman to be so honored.
December 1955	*Teacher*, Helen's biography about Anne Sullivan Macy, is published.
Winter 1956–57	William Gibson's play *The Miracle Worker*, based on Helen's early life with Anne, debuts on television and on Broadway.
May 1957	Helen and Polly tour Iceland and Scandinavia.
March 21, 1960	Polly Thomson dies.
October 1961	Helen suffers her first stroke and retires from public life.
September 1964	President Lyndon Johnson confers the Presidential Medal of Freedom, the nation's highest civilian honor, upon Helen. She is unable to attend the ceremony.
June 1, 1968	Helen Keller passes away in her sleep. Over 1,200 mourners attend the funeral at the National Cathedral. Helen's ashes are interred there with those of Anne and Polly.
Addendum September 11, 2001	Helen Keller International Headquarters are severely damaged in the terrorist attacks on the twin Towers in New York, New York. Eighty-five years of priceless archives of Helen Keller papers, books, and other items are lost. Several items do survive, including a "singed" terra cotta bust of Helen, presented to her on her first trip to Japan in 1937.

October 7, 2009   A life size sculpture depicting Helen Keller as a young girl at the pump in Ivy Green, Alabama, is installed in Statuary Hall, US Capitol, Washington DC, as one of two statues representing the state of Alabama. It is the first depiction of a child and also a disabled person in that historic setting. Utah artist Edward Hlavka was commissioned to create the Helen Keller sculpture.

The Myth of Water

Practicing Speech

Onboard the Asama Maru, 1937

Here on shipboard
the speeches must be practiced
or few will understand me.
I begin
and then my heart sinks.
The speeches do not please.
They must be short,
not overtax my listeners.
My delivery halts,
I am anxious.
I want to plead
for the words
that move beyond
deaf boundaries, for hope
that shines
past darkness . . .

I stop, gulp air.
Relax, Helen.

Relax your throat,
remember
the supple neck
of the opera singer
whose fine movement
you felt—taut skin
and muscle, the tender
vibrato, bones
precise machinery.

   I am told
there are high notes
that ease the soul
to ecstasy, and base
notes that resonate with power.
I feel their levels
as a bird wing pulls flight.

For now, I content myself
with dull practice—
move my tongue and lips
as Teacher drilled me,
push out air, remembering
to breathe as I
will the sound
from this mechanical jaw.
I speak for *her.*

I keep my face lifted,
forward. My message
simple, not world—

2

shaking. Just hope
for the sight of unborn children,
a meaningful job
for the blinded veteran,
that we know an answer
to the question *What then*
shall we do? is within
our grasp, our sight.

The poem recalls Helen's trip to Japan on the Asama Maru, from San Francisco, just six months after Anne Sullivan Macy's death to meet the deaf-blind and encourage preventing blindness. There are many accounts of Keller's frustration over trying to perfect normal speech, yet she was determined to communicate with audiences that way. It also refers to several instances when she "heard" music by singers that are well-documented in the literature. The scriptural reference, "And now what shall we do?" (Luke 3:1–22), is the emblematic question for Helen, as she worked for the American Foundation for the Blind at home and abroad to fight blindness and to find meaningful work for the blind and deaf-blind.

I

You are Helen

1880–1917

After her graduation from Radcliff (cum laude) in 1904, Keller and Anne Sullivan purchased a farm at Wrentham, Massachusetts. A year later Sullivan married John Macy, who helped Keller edit her first two books. During this time Peter Fagan, a man seven years Keller's junior, began working as a secretary to Keller, Sullivan, and John Macy. Keller and Fagan began a love affair in Wrentham that concluded unhappily in Montgomery, Alabama, when their plan to elope was either foiled or abandoned. Overlapping with her time in Montgomery from fall 1916 until later in 1917, Keller was also separated for about five months from Teacher who convalesced from exhaustion and respiratory disease in Puerto Rico. While Keller was a public figure in her sister's hometown, she struggled to reconcile lost love and temporary separation from Teacher. When Sullivan returned in 1917, they sold Wrentham and moved to New York.

Love is what animates all life—it is not outside of us—
separate from us. It *is* us.

—Helen Keller, from *My Religion*

Memory of Ivy Green

Tuscumbia, Alabama

The first time I entered a wave
   my feet swept up under me
      by a force stronger than wind
or Mother's arms—
   nothing held me—

The salt water touched me
      like an earlier time, featureless air,
a bland surging engulfed me,
   just a babe—who could know
      anything of loneliness or death?
I was alone, tumbling
   in the deep element of myself.

When my little feet found no bottom,
   no sand scratched my toes—
      I was
cut lose—returned to an elemental pulse—
   with no thought of exit,
      or birth.

ℰ ℰ ℰ

Flickering leaves
   played across the bathroom floor—
      I toddled forward, arms outstretched—
Then this—
   the receding sound of Mother's
breath at the phantom's ear—
These she cannot claim,

they are not hers,

        language has not taken her—
    little soul cast off into the deep
    ocean of herself,
        no mooring, no anchor.

Keller commented that she felt during the time before language as if she were "a vacancy absorbing space" (*A Light in My Darkness*). The scene she said she remembered prior to her illness was when she first walked, about age one, in the bathroom at Ivy Green.

First Dream of the Tennessee

There is a river in Alabama I remember—those rocks
　　my feet found, with her hand steadying me to that current's
cold muscle taking me this way and that.
　　Sun on my face, my hair lifted the mud's ancient odor,
said *move with me.*

I cannot return to who I was. In the garden of my home place
　　I had groped without self, without *Helen*, only *need*
and *want.* When Teacher dragged this phantom
　　to the pump and poured w-a-t-e-r into its impatient hand,
my mind cracked, like a bird's egg. This
　　I try to tell—but you can never know. I was
diving into that name.
　　I couldn't know then . . . Still, my feet steadied
on bare rocks, knew the river's rich pull.

How would it be possible
　　to return there, the syllables whispering in my palm
over and over, *you are Helen, of this Earth.*

In Keller's biography of Anne Sullivan Macy, *Teacher*, she refers to herself as *Phantom*, indicating the time before Teacher introduced her to words and began her real education. The pump-house apprehension of the word "w-a-t-e-r" was the turning point, though Keller writes that she did not understand all of language at that point.

At Wrentham

1914

At Wrentham, I learn the firs,
how days arrange themselves to ease
and seize us. *A mourning dove*
gives up the night, Teacher says. Above,
a plucked vine quivers. Sweet, these.

My best friend's husband, beset
by fever to escape—leaves, returns, teases
her. Then you appear, spelling *I am here*
at Wrentham.

The world I know scatters like leaves
torn by storm from the trees, but a choice
shelters me. I learn a song composed of
days attuned for love—
believe a woman could be free
at Wrentham.

Keller, Sullivan, and John Macy spent several happy years at the farm at Wrentham,
Massachusetts. Macy edited Keller's writing, but soon he and Sullivan separated.
During this time, Peter Fagan was hired as a secretary to help with correspondence;
he and Keller fell in love.

This Day

To Peter Fagan

Into my hand the stars poured light
    and I knew you,
                or so I thought.
There was no way for you to know my darkness,
    understand my silence, but you persisted with your
questions, probing.
                You shook language
    in my face and asked me to dance syntax
with you. Dark dancer, I followed your lead,
    and if you could have seen what I knew
through our touch, we would've been one!

The night comes, I dress, remember my valise,
         and quietly work my way down the stairs
guided by your presence in me. Alabama
    again is a place to flee.
              Alone on Sister's front porch,
without Teacher, scent of tea olive lingering, your promises
    fade into morning's traffic, until you are no more
        than a rumble from the street
signaling day.
        Let loss, only loss,
guide me. *Not to be yours,*
    Helen, not to be yours, this day.

Silence

Montgomery, Alabama, 1916

I listen to the pin oak, waiting
    for any sign of you, the notice of Teacher's

hand pressing your letter into mine
    from your pen-scratched ink

spells your blood and bone motion in my palm.
    The oak's movement in the faltering breeze

makes a language I try to translate, roots
    studying the depths of earth,

bark ungiving, rough branches
    moving as if cracked off

by the wind. My boot-toe snags a loop.
    I will not stop listening to this tree,

overgrown with herself and filled with
    her coursing thoughts and murmurs. How

can I turn away from such offers?
    You are silent. If I never learn

one fraction more of your soul's equation—
    you I know.

From the deep beneath me
    the tree holds herself still.

The letter you do not send, the ink erases
    itself, Teacher's hand rests curled, cupped

in her palm. I press fingers against the nubbled bark that spells
an unintelligible line like I sometimes remember doing

when I awaken.

"This Day" and "Silence" recall Keller's love affair and failed attempt to elope with
Peter Fagan from Felder Avenue in November 1916, in Montgomery, Alabama.

Teacher's Letter from Puerto Rico

"I go to bed every night soaked with sunshine and orange
blossoms, and fall to sleep to the soporific sound of oxen
munching banana leaves."
—Anne Sullivan Macy, letter to Helen Keller, 1917

I translated the world for you.
Here you need no translation.
In tropical rain and heat,
wake or dream, free of both you and me.

Here you need no translation,
here the sun drenches the senses—
Free of us both,
the stars pour out for me like wine.

Here the sun drenches all—
I am open, alive.
I wake to the stars' heat,
birds' tongues

and good health freely given,
like rain, in the stars,
touch, speaking easily
as birds sing in later afternoon light.

How did we grow so far from ourselves, Helen?

Our fingers could read

our moist life like the Psalms.

Easy touch—

the island waking.

I am free here, free and consoled.

"Teacher's Letter from Puerto Rico" is a modified pantoum based loosely on correspondence between Keller and Anne Sullivan Macy while Sullivan was in Puerto Rico (1917) for convalescence from lung disease. This was one of the longest periods of separation for Keller and Teacher in their life together.

Soliloquy

Palm Sunday 1917

Just tell them, The Lord needs it—just tell them.
It's a simple task you perform.
Today without you I am as useless as a broken pot.

Outside Jerusalem today they went looking without Jesus for a colt.
Could this unbroken animal teach them?
Just tell them, The Lord needs it.

Cutting palms, they spread the branches for his feet.
I know those feet, and how they make me turn.
Today, without you, I am as useless.

Today we are called to the passion, to believe—
Even a woman, alone, can claim,
Just tell them, The Lord needs it.

I was walking with them, spreading sharp
palm fronds for his feet. I was happy, hopeless, crying,
Today without you, *I am.*

With you there was an island of joy, but here my heart
widens sorrow where I would be freed. There will be freedom
today without you, *one I loved.*
Just tell them, the Lords needs it.

In her memoir *Midstream* (1929), Keller refers to her brief love affair with Peter Fagan as a "little island of joy." Two lines of scripture inform the poem. "Just tell them, the Lord needs it." (Luke 19:31) and "I am as useless as a broken pot." (Psalm 31:12).

Imaginary Letter to John Hitz

1917

The greatest word of Jesus to His disciples is *abandon*.
This is a line I caught today from one of your meditations.
That someone would think of a single
greatest word of Jesus clarifies the world.

This is a line I caught today from one of your meditations
about *abandon* releases the world—
a greatest word that clarifies Jesus
then goes on to clear a path for us.

About *abandon* and *release*, the world
can never agree, never resolve or abide.
The word clears a path for us.
About the earth's touch, its taste, its very smell, we

can never agree, never resolve or abide.
Each day you send me a meditation
about the earth's touch, its taste, its very smell.
We exchange words like this, pierced in paper.

Each day you send me a meditation.
In this way I can abandon the world.
I read your words on my fingertips.
That someone would think of a single word—

The greatest word of Jesus to His disciples is *abandon*.

Hitz was a spiritual mentor to Keller from the time she was a young girl and this is
an imagined meditation addressed to him.

Encounter in Montgomery

1917

Walking in Sister's yard, I found a plant I couldn't name—
the foliage billowed like nothing I knew, frothed
in plumes with tiniest bracts—asparagus? No, *celery*,
I exclaimed. But, it wasn't. When I put my face
into the spray, it was cool on my eyelids,
a spring of delicate mist. Teacher might say,
Within each plume a blush of rust suggests itself,
then hides in the cloud of green. I didn't expect
a plant that felt like coolest peace, without a leaf
discernible, with only the sketch of itself to breathe.
Oh, the fennel, Sister said, later. And I knew
the fragrant pillow of it was as tangible
as the thought of him I had let go, let drift out
and away.

An imagined scene at the home of Mildred Keller Tyson on Felder Avenue in Montgomery as Keller resolves her grief over Peter Fagan.

The Little Boy Next Door

*After a black and white photograph of Helen with
an unidentified child*

I knew first from a distance his ramble across the yard
    toward the porch to sit with me on the rock wall:
his smell of infant sweat and something else, a milk
    musk mixed with his mother's talc
and the dark rich dirt from the backyard arbor.
    He played there late. When I moved
in my garden, touching the rose trees to shake their
    fragrance at close of day, he ran
quickly to nestle against my skirt, his small dumb
    hand patting my thigh to signal, *I am here.*

One day a visitor thought to photograph us
    and so we posed as I imagine a mother
and child do for a memory book. His warm, damp
    body next to me, he pressed his head against
my breast with a quiet knowledge, let me finger
    his toes to feel dust powered there and learn
where he had played.
                I was younger then,
    and felt the quickening of a mother's desire for his
small body on hers.
              Later, when you did not arrive
to take me from Alabama, I mourned the child lost
to me. There would be no difference to lose him—one I would
    never have—or that child, pressed from my body,
the dark smell rising to tell me at last who I am.

II

BRIDGE
Helen Keller's Journal, 1936–1937

A widely published writer whose *The Story of My Life* was an international bestseller when she was just out of college in 1904, Keller began a personal journal in November 1936 to assuage her grief at the loss of her friend and companion Anne Sullivan Macy whom she affectionately called "Teacher." Begun just a few weeks after Sullivan's death, the entries chronicle her travels to Scotland, England, and France, and her return to Forest Hills, Long Island, New York, before setting sail for Japan and Korea. Polly Thomson, a close friend who stepped in as fulltime companion when Sullivan died, accompanied Keller on this trip. The journal concludes April 14, 1937, thus covering the first six months of mourning Teacher's loss and the bridge to Keller's expanded life as a world ambassador for the deaf-blind.

She made every word vibrant to my mind—she would not let the silence about me be *silent*.

—Helen Keller, from *Teacher: Anne Sullivan Macy*

First Entry, after Midnight

November 4, 1936
Aboard the SS Deutschland, en route for England

What I haven't written I will now: the sorrow cannot be
shaped into a metaphor as I try cheating sharp grief:
the deepest sorrow knows no time—
It seems an eternal night. The truth is—words slip
under my fingers like the typewriter on this listing ship.
But a sentence can link me to her, a rope of breath I smelled
in a dream, her perfume hovering over me. Standing tall,
my face forward, I please the photographer as our journey starts.
Most of the time I appear to myself to be a somnambulist,
impelled only by an intense Faith. Faith, I test you now,
like all grief does. *It is sweet because it helps me*
to cross halfway with Teacher into her new life,
. . . terrible because it drives me to think of others' sorrow
before my own, to hold up the torch of hope for the blind

when tears blot out all the stars for me.
To perform one task after another when the joy of work is fled . . . .
I write a page, and stop. Words crumble into chaotic
    sticks. That place before a word taught me to know her.

With excerpts from *Helen Keller's Journal* in italics and images from observations
in the first week, this entry is imagined.

The Not-You

November 1936

You are near, Teacher!
There is a space I circle,
speaking the letters in my own hand
like a stumbling freak lost again.
In that space I circle
the not-you, the nowhere, absence
letting me hear you come close—
I can hear you come close—
Let me feel you all around me—
that will be enough—
Death burns the eye,
death opens true—
you are free now—
Now you've released me—
Like my own hand numbed from me.
Who hears me?
Torn from me, you are near.

"The Not-You" and "Another Country" are set just two weeks after Anne Sullivan Macy's death when Keller and Polly Thomson, her companion and assistant, embarked on an overseas trip to Scotland, Thomson's homeland, and then to Asia. The well-known travel reference in "Another Country" is from Ralph Waldo Emerson's *Self-Reliance.*

Another Country

November 1936

On shipboard Polly told me
how the gulls circled,
hovered, the white sea swallows
close behind. You
could have been right beside us, Teacher.

In our compartment now
on the train to Scotland
I wake from a dream
and reach for your hand,
you can lend your clear words
to the autumn air I smell—
fields, falling leaves.

I thought
another country
might erase the pain,
but we carry ourselves, always,
alone when we travel.
I believe I see you
right beside us, friend!
Like the swallows
flying a thousand miles out to sea,
wise or foolish,
with no thought of time,
I fly,
grope deaf—
blind a second time.

Dream of the Manse
Children Talking

The Manse, Scotland, December 1936

Stubby Fingers lurches
out simple words. I smell him
as he thinks what to say
to the woman holding out
a strange, open hand to hear.
His brother, lithe and fragile-fingered,
skitters out sentences that roll and toss.
He resembles a deer in the forest
racing through moonlight.

Their fingers touch my lips
and I read words there,
the manual alphabet
dissolving to tiny taps of their
fingertips against
my face. No need to corral
all this in the orderly palm
of my mind, we are gleeful
in this discovery. We are
practically singing to
one another.
We are singing.
Yes, we are singing!

Several journal entries chronicle Keller's delight over children who finger-spelled
with her in Scotland.

The Exquisite Instrument
That Makes an Ear

Central Hotel, Glasgow, December 23, 1936

This morning I woke, positive I had seen Teacher,
dreamed she was driving with Polly and me
through a countryside resembling our home at South Arcan
with heather-plumed hills and hawthorn-bloom
rolling from hedge to hedge.
          She glowed with health
and the joy of finding me so close to her.
She looked and looked as if she could not have enough
of looking about us. She gave me an exquisite
instrument, saying, *Listen, Helen, and this*
will be an ear for you. It will rain sounds upon your hand—
song-birds, passing footsteps from afar, murmuring
water you cannot reach. Another of your fetters
will be broken.
              A caress—and she was gone.

An almost entirely found poem, this event is quoted by Kim E. Nielson in *Helen Keller: Selected Writings.*

Fragment of an Afternoon
at Musee Rodin, Paris,
with Gutzon Borglum

January 30, 1937

The large figure,
situated in the garden
among tightly pruned
plants screaming
for release
A seated man,
chin in hand,
pushing out thought
as an act of will

Suddenly in
Alabama
at the pump,
body releasing
one word, then
the next
until a stream
of thought
shatters my palm
The energy of it
leaves me outside
myself, my hand
alive with the thought
of *me, her,*
every object
has a name

At home will I
be a ghost with
bare fingers
touching
a book,
a cotton shawl, the figure
of a young woman
in stone, asking for
Teacher,
my hand
a blank slate,
grief
a surface
scored with light and dark

In her journal Keller confesses a dread of returning to the house in New York without Anne Sullivan Macy and also describes her visit to the Musee Rodin while in Paris. The sculptor Gutzon Borglum arranged for her to manually view Rodin's "The Thinker" and other works. This poem attempts to braid two emotional states.

Enrico Caruso Remembers Helen Keller

1918

> *The Georgian Terrance Hotel, Atlanta. Interior. Day.*
> *Caruso speaking, as if to no one.*

I tell you, I have recorded this voice on wax,
have let scientists explore my throat
searching for the lyric tenor's throbbing birdsong,
but never felt a soul enter as you did
when those keen fingers hovered on my lips, and
my breath, vibrato inscribed them. I swear the whirls
of your fingertips would play back the aria
if a needle could set their grooves.
Vois ma misere, helas. See my misery, alas,
all analogy fails me—
I am just a man who interprets song,
gives breath to notes, life to words—
but when I held your strong wrist,
your finger's pulse at my lips, I knew an audience
with God—
Afterwards, I turned away, couldn't catch my breath.
(Had you taken it?) I know you swooned.
No applause, no *Bravo! Bravo!*
will touch me again as you did—
I have sung the best for you in my life, Helen Keller.

Sailing home in 1937 after visiting Paris and immersing herself in the arts, Keller recalled her April 24, 1916, visit with world-famous tenor Enrico in Atlanta. According to news accounts, Caruso sang the opening aria of the third act from Saint-Saens's *Samson et Delilah* to Keller as she manually read his lips, thus translating French as well as lip-reading with her fingers.

Returnings

Early Spring, 1937

1. Aboard the SS Champlain, February 9, 1937
Ship's Deck. Exterior. Day.

Has faith, then, proved a mockery?
Where is the message Teacher sent to me?
Has faith, then, proved a mockery
saying, *open your hand?*
Nothing speaks to me.

Yet it is as if she never left.
She does not speak to me.
I will touch the chair
as if she never left . . .
I have been too close to death.

2. Home, Forest Hills, Long Island, NY, February 10, 1937
Interior. Night. Dreaming.

A chair, her books, how the room opens for me—
I feel her reach against the fading light.
Fifty years she conjured words for me.
Who leans in *now?*
Pain dares me, locks my fingers against themselves . . .
this fight!
I know she reaches out against the fading light.

Keller's return voyage to the United States. from Europe was colored by her antic-
ipation of returning to the house without Teacher. Once home, Keller found Sul-
livan's spirit everywhere.

Imaginary Farewell from Russell Cone to Helen Keller

The Golden Gate, traveling to the Far East,
    April 1, 1937

Ma'am, you see it was good work
because it was safe work—hard hats,
no drinking allowed. One stunt
at any height
and they were off the job.
But the best we gave them
was the net. Suspended
under the bridge, like under a circus tent,
designed to
catch a man, a can of paint,
a ton of scaffolding.

On that morning eleven men
worked the platform, prepared steel
for the orange vermillion
to paint her right into
the California landscape.
On the north tower
two men already in the net
scraping away debris.

Like a big sigh, five tons
of scaffolding
gave way and hung crazily,
tilting the men to the water below—
then all fell to the net

36

like babes into a mother's
outstretched apron.
The relief we felt you can imagine,
a moment's joy.
The tearing we heard next
was like a machine gun's crack
or the rip of a picket fence splintering.
All down—men, wood, net
220 feet into water
you now cross.

Twelve fell, two lived.
One man knocked unconscious
by a piece of lumber then
shocked back to life
in the icy channel.
Strong swimmer, tangled
underwater, he made it, broken,
lived to tell so I can tell you, Miss Keller,
the worker is never
truly safe. One man builds
so another can cross.

March 26–31, Keller and Polly Thomson traveled overland by train from New York
by way of Chicago to Kansas City to San Francisco where they boarded the Asama
Maru on April 1 to sail for Japan and Korea. Moving under the newly opened
Golden Gate Bridge, Keller remembered workers killed during its construction.
Much of the imagery comes from an historical account of constructing the Golden
Gate by the project manager, Russell Cone.

River, Bridge, and Sky

Aboard the Asama Maru, North Pacific Ocean,
April 14, 1937

At 6 A.M. a mist floated around the ship
like incense from a burner.
Polly and I take our last walk
on deck. Both silent, we know
what the other is thinking—
this is Teacher's birthday.
We practice the speeches,
ready ourselves to pose.

"Plucking the flower of life,"
the Chinese say of death.
Today, I think of you as a lotus flower,
opening in the morning with curving petals
and leaves whose surfaces reflect
every mood of sky. I think
of those who will say behind their hands,
She who doesn't know light,
much less a flower, writes this?

Before we set sail, a gift:
the cast of your hand.
Reaching for
what I knew I could never
find again—*that electric touch—*
the thumb and index finger
forming the letter *L*—
I traced

each line in your palm,
startlingly distinct and true.

Teacher, you made a path for me.
A small, well-tended
garden, with turns
for river, bridge and sky.

The world knows
you opened my hand
and names flew into the air.
But who can know
how you touched me
with your sight—
Begged me
to enter a land you
promised I would see.

Partially found and partially imagined, the reference to the cast of Anne Sullivan
Macy's hand, the lotus, and the garden come from *Helen Keller's Journal*, entries in
March and April, just before the trip to Japan.

I Promised

Arriving Japan, 1937

I would step on this island,
touch the lips
of deaf-blind women.

You said *make this trip for me—*
your last command
laid in my heart's open palm—

tap-tap of *yes*
obliterates the timid sweep,
no

Arriving here, I think,
I cannot fly from place
to place looking for you.

I turn around
and my words explode
like river birds.

Helen Keller promised Sullivan on her deathbed that she would take their public
service work for the deaf-blind to Japan and Korea.

III

Your Light

1943–1948

From 1943 to 1948 Keller visited an estimated seventy hospitals, giving encouragement to wounded veterans blinded or maimed in WWII, calling this work, "The crowning experience of my life." In 1948, Keller made her second trip to the Far East, witnessing the devastation of the nuclear bombs in Hiroshima and Nagasaki. Thousands greeted them at every stop, and, reportedly, children sang songs written for Keller.

For many years I have sensed profoundly the war-made wrongs and crookedness of mankind, but now it is more than a feeling, it is a concrete knowledge I have gained, a stern resolve to work for the breaking of barbarism and the fostering of universal peace.

—Helen Keller. Letter to Nella Brady Henley,
October, 14, 1948, from Japan

From a Japanese Child
along the Parade Route

Hiroshima, October 1948

Our teachers have asked us
to greet you, to show respect,
a friend of our country.
Champion of the blind, a woman
who cannot hear, you speak to us
from your American heart.

For eleven years I obeyed
my parents, honored
ancestors. Now all my family
rests in the one grave, instantly gone.
What news can you bring us
from your country?

You look sad beside the woman
who tells you with her fingers
what we say. She looks as if she
would break into a thousand pieces.
Does she miss her country?

I would hold your hand,
you could touch my face
(I am not scarred), carry home
one soft, unwounded touch,
a gift to your country.

Reproach

Hiroshima, with Takeo Iwahashi, 1948

The faces of those I touch
are like the broken rubble under my steps.
I cannot get my bearings.
Takeo stops speaking . . .
In my own silence I know

nothing is said—Polly's fingers
spell in my upturned hand: *no sound*
but a small choking for breath.
Bomb. Ash. Seared face.
Here in Hiroshima, beautiful city I visited
so soon after Teacher's death, found
people's grace, such welcome.
I breathe the flesh of the gardenia
the welfare officer pins to my jacket.
When I touch his face,
his expression a mask of disbelief.
My country did this
I have touched the blinded soldier,
the knee stump *My country did this*
and now I stumble on this earth.

Takeo Iwahashi was a dear friend of Helen's and Teacher's who first extended an invitation to visit prior to Teacher's death. The notion of *reproach* is taken from Helen's letter to Nella Brady Henley on October 14, 1948, about Helen and Polly Thomson's trip to Japan and their visits to the bomb sites and meetings with survivors.

Late Elegy for FDR

Japan, October 1948

I carry you with me as I move among these people,
    wondering, would you have done this?
In the naval hospitals I saw our wounded, wanted
    to give them hope, a loving touch. One soldier said,
"Now that I have felt your kiss, I can live!"
    Friend, you led us to hope.

In the wards, I felt the scrape of a wheel chair,
    the ominous thud of a gurney lifted,
flat wool blankets where a stump met my fingers.
    Their uplifted faces cheered, someone said, by my words—
They couldn't know how they honored me with their presence.
    Here in this country, seared past recognition,
horror masks faces, children sing,
                    I move among them
    and wonder, could you have done this?

An avowed pacifist and longtime friend of Eleanor and Franklin Roosevelt, Helen might have reasonably wondered if the recently deceased President would've done the same as President Truman to end the war.

First Light at the Shinto Shrine for A.S.M.

Miyajima, Japan, October 1948

>—*news reel of Helen lighting a candle for Teacher*

This morning the doctor shows me the stone wall of a hospital,
    leaning like a reed in the wind from the concussive blast.
Facts and beauty tumble together. They call me *Saint*, but why?
    Because I am deaf-blind, because I learned
to speak like a rough machine? After the long day,
    jolting car rides, the ruined, staring faces Polly saw,
and vibrations of the children clapping hands, I feel Teacher
    rise up, saying, "Helen, it is time for peace. Open your heart!"
I place flowers at the little shrine, then a guiding hand
    puts a candle in mine, urges me to begin your light.
We will not let her flame go out, someone spells to me.
    I accept peace the way I drink water, know your spirit,
Teacher. I turn back to the world now.
    Peace possible, your light.

IV

COMING THROUGH FIRE

Circa 1955

Helen recalls moments of illumination with Teacher in Alabama and grapples with the sacrifice Anne Sullivan Macy made for her pupil to fully know the world. Helen pictures the fire in 1948 at Arcan Ridge, Connecticut, in which cherished Braille books, personal papers and letters, and mementoes of a lifetime, including Helen and Teacher's personal Braille correspondence and three quarters of a first manuscript of *Teacher*, perished. For Helen, Teacher was both friend and conduit—most of all she was the one who opened the world of knowing, and brought Helen to herself. Some images arise from *Teacher: Anne Sullivan Macy* (1955) and some are imagined.

Hands so quiet, folded on a book—
Hands forgetful of words they have read all night,
Hands asleep on the open page.

—Fragment of poem by Anne Sullivan Macy, quoted in *Teacher*

Hunger

I . . . think of her as a spirit giving warmth, a sun of life.
—Helen Keller, *Teacher*

One morning at home by the Tennessee River, that giant,
    she said *I am going to show you light, a gull wing in a mussel shell.*
A silver slip of mussel shell beneath my fingertip
    telling me the glint of summer light.
Numberless shells on the shoreline washed up where we walked.
    Hold this, she spelled, and dropped the rough halves
of a pebbled one, broken open, into my hand. *Gray*, she said, *like old*
    men, crustaceans of inner life. We rinsed the shells, dried them in our
        petticoats.
Mud, she said, *blackening the white linen.* We didn't care, grit beneath
    fingernails quickened touch. *Turn it over, touch here and feel the opal,*
she said, *the satin curve where the animal grips. Swipe past the sharp edge.*
The smoothness you feel, Helen, is how light presents itself, that sudden.
We touched that secret side of mussel shell warming in Alabama sun.
    How it drew us there, spreading bounty on flat rocks.

Another time, opening the door to a screened porch on Mobile Bay,
    facing west, we breathed the hot sponge blur of briny air,
lemon-scent from last night's shrimp boil. She saw a gull winging.
    A slip opening, wings catching light, Helen! she spelled. *Remember the*
mussel shell, that smoothness? That is the gull wing, opening, catching
light the way your fingertip caught the opal fire.

Word-hunger, light-hunger
                    haunt me without you, my teacher.

Teacher

The numberless mussel shells, mother of pearl slip under my fingertip,
    the shimmering Alabama summer heat, the pull of white gull wing
on Mobile Bay in that swipe of opal. Branches of blue fir rising
    above me at Wrentham in summer, lifting up and up. Body
of the Southern Magnolia, its fragrance heavy as philosophy,
    its fleshy petals real as birth. I wanted to run my hands over it—
the blooms wide open books. *The color of rich cream*, she said,
    of my lover's neck.

And there was the fired poured into me, the words searing my palm
    as gently as a trapped bird whirring, a vibration I felt at Ivy Green
when swallows beat their wings against the stone chimney.
    Strike that fire of knowing, Helen, your mind wants to fly free.
Does knowing bring an echo to silence that refuses? *Bird trill*, she said,
    is the pulse here, pressing my fingertip to my wrist. *That beating*
point is the note. Bird cadence when dawn erupts, like fingers on your bare
    shoulders, breeze in your hair, at your elbow. I knew it true as fire.
Later, at Wrentham, there was a whiff of charred paper from the fireplace.
    Teacher said, *I have burned my journal.* (Words erased by fire
after they'd burned from a pen?)
                        Years later, a blaze took everything
at Arcan Ridge—letters, diaries, a draft of Teacher's life—all melted
    into unchanging blackness. I was glad, fumbling to tell it again, say
    no, no,
across my palm, urging tender to spark, the word-hunger
    she held out to me, igniting. Lifting me out of myself
like the newborn's eye cleared by drops of silver nitrate,
    waging God's war against darkness.

One Word

My fingers across your face moments
    after the temperature in your palm
dropped below the life line—knew you were gone.
    This is not Teacher! I cried to anyone who could hear.
In our attic study, I held that touch
    of soul-empty flesh. In bright sun
by the window where you had read to me,
    I wanted to speak you back to warmth,
soft contour of the soul's shadow.

Alone then, I knew the opiate fog returning,
    a slow movement through water
when light first receded, my ears closed over stone.
    You had opened all with one word: first *doll*,
then *water* claimed me

                and I was yours.

Our Hands

The words you burned, words lost at random,
    none catch your particular fire,
the cadence of letters spilled to words I cupped, a gift,
    your vision. *No one recognizes the light*, you wrote.
I know when I cross over, I will find you alive,
    sighted. You who never dreamed your life would be
leading a deaf-blind girl to names, things. You gave me
    the world, myself—

How can I bear the burden of this sacrifice, Teacher?
    I see us: the dip of a gull wing
glints opal in sunlight   where we walk out
    holding words in our minds,
                our hands touching what they will.

V

Tell the World

1950–Present Day

As she traveled the world on behalf of the American Foundation for the Overseas Blind, Helen continued to experience the world as few have, including the diversity of arts and multiculturalism. The American sculptor Jo Davidson took her to Florence, Italy, and Helen made a well-documented visit to the Martha Graham Dance Company in New York City in 1954. Exhorting leaders and the powerful to work for the deaf-blind, Helen left a legacy of advocacy that resonates well into the twenty-first century. She died just before her eighty-eighth birthday in 1968.

You are so accustomed to light, I fear you will stumble when I try to guide you through the land of darkness and silence.

—Helen Keller, from *The World I Live In*

Jo Davidson's Letter from Florence, Italy

In the Bargello and Medici Tombs, with Helen, 1950

It's true, she felt form as no sculptor I've ever known.
Her hand passed lightly with an intimate knowledge across
the master's David. Though I gazed one hundred hours on that work,
measured the large hand with my eyes, the proportions of the face,
she knew the interplay of light on flesh, the way incision
casts a shadow.
            She gathered in each muscle
of Donatello's youth as if she caught the smell of flesh
through bronze. We led her to the Tombs, then she led us.
Watching her from below, transfixed, we saw her hands travel
over "Night" and "Dawn." The form must have risen
to her touch with knowledge complete, without boundary,
as the poet's line explodes forth when words find their body.

Alone on the scaffolding, she left us, entered a world
only she could inhabit—and even this is not accurate—
how can we know who she was at that moment?
                             What she became?

Internationally known American sculptor Jo Davidson arranged for Keller to manually view masterpieces by Donatello and Michelangelo in Florence, Italy. He documents this in his self-published autobiography *Between Sittings* (1950).

Helen's Meditation in the Marble Quarry, Carrara, Italy

Spring 1950

After the shaking bus climbed and climbed
to Carrara, we boarded a wagon for the trip
inside the mountain's deeper dark
cool air. Others around me shuddered,
almost afraid. In the stone vault, the ceiling
soared above us like a cathedral.
I knew how a crevice reveals
    cool stone as a shadow changes
from sunlight to shade.
        This is elemental. Any child can know it.

The master came here to quarry stone
for a pope's tomb, searched months
for the purest white stone without a vein.
How he must have raged!
What I felt was peace, surrounded by rock
    he would tear until it became human,
coaxing from it *life*. I was matter,

encased in a stone's cell, waiting
for the precise chisel of her fingers
in my palm. This is the way music comes to me,
    pulsation of air, notes bombarding,
a life force demanding ecstasy
or terror, as private as the fluttering

of bird wings,
　　or a lover's breath
suddenly warm at my ear.

This companion to the Jo Davidson monologue imagines Helen's tour of a marble quarry at Carrara from which Michelangelo famously selected stone for his masterworks.

With the Martha Graham Dance Company

New York 1954

> —*Helen is filmed and photographed meeting and dancing with Graham and the Company*

To move on feet like these requires a different sight.
The floor shook. With a new rhythm of their footfalls
and the lift of their toes, I knew their vibrant light.

The small one, their master whose very body spelled *breath*,
guided me to a young man, a gnarled foot I held.
To move on feet like these requires a different sight.

His toes pointing the urge to be up and up, that height,
the subtle heat of their bodies, their movement called.
With the lift of their toes, I knew their vibrant light.

When she pulled me into them, a current ran, spear-like,
tightening, as if my whole body were a palm.
To move on feet like these requires a different sight.

My sturdy shoes on that elastic floor knew joy uplifted
and she—rod-straight and lithe, her body hard, a calm
praise for the lift of their toes, that vibrant life—

She sheared around us—a star, a comet whose bright
corona poured forth joy's spoken filaments. All
to move on feet like these—a different sight!
To know the lift of their toes, I moved in their vibrant light.

In Which Helen Puts to Rest the Mirror

Polished glass reflects anything before it.
I was taught to foxtrot, smile with grace,
portray the blind freed from fear.
Fear, that fleeting partner who found me, locked,
immobile before the mirror.

How can she know her beauty? tell her flaws?
learn how age lights on her
without my persuading echo?
I opened my palm to listen,
Teacher spelled,

"The lake reflects the trees real
as when God made them, perfect as a mirror."
Love on my face, what was that?
Loss in my heart, what was that?
Reflect these? Why would I want a mirror?

The children's fingers, like wildflowers,
tell the world true as glass reflects silence in a mirror.
When you cross to the next room after death, Helen,
the light is yours, the birdsong clear.
You'll know, without the mirror.

Based loosely on actress Georgette LeBlanc's *The Girl Who Found the Bluebird:
A Visit to Helen Keller*, and Helen's accounts of her own faith about life after death.

What Helen Saw / What Helen Said

—*After Cynthia Ozick's "What Helen Keller Saw,"*
The New Yorker, *June 16 and 23, 2003.*

A child, they would not let me write,
take a pen or punch paper for my own thoughts.
I knew what I knew, knew what I saw.
Detractors and doubters thrilled

at any misstep. So I misstepped
and stepped again
into the widening field of my own awakening.
Once, still a child, I quoted another's story

given to me. A jury of adults cried *reprobate.*
When I told a sunset, I was branded a fool,
or worse, but I say no poet cared
more for a true line than I.

On my passport I selected *author.*
Listening to Teacher's brilliant fingers fly
telling me the professor's words so I might
write the exam alone, I had no fear. Language

buoyed me up like the sleekest sloop. They said
I couldn't chart a course because I couldn't read
a sextant, see the stars' position, or know a true horizon.
I laughed in God's ear when they said, "What she

writes is a lie, someone told her how the world
looks and what creation seems to be." Did anger turn

red in the mind's eye, can the skin's blush be far from
the tenderness I felt when he touched my hand

saying, *I will take care of you, I love you.*
Is telling the world just a matter of seeing a paint box?
Language is my anchor and threshold. Pity souls
who use words to flog the lost, the deaf, the silent girl.

The Myth of W-a-t-e-r

It was not a single word and there was no utterance.
You may have your play, your frozen moment in time
if these please you. But understand, Teacher lead me
to the well house to distinguish between *water* and what
holds it for drinking. I held the cup under the pump and she
wrenched the handle. I could smell her sweat, though
I didn't know its name—only that it mixed with the garden
and told me she was near. The liquid hit my fingers
where I gripped the cup's handle—in my other upturned palm
she spelled the letters over and over, like fire.
There was a moment when everything came,
that my mind accepted thought like a body
crossing a threshold through the opened door.
It was illumination and joy, then more words until *Teacher,
Helen, world, go. Go into your life!*

CODA

In Terra Cotta

Present day

> "Bust of Helen Keller One of Three
> Artifacts Saved in 9/11 Fire"
> —news headline

Can you see my likeness now?
Touch the singed face,
think how the slow anneal
of re-fired clay is like the return
of those souls to the One
who made them.
You have the World
to consider.

In 1937, a Japanese artist presented Helen with a terra cotta bust of herself when she visited Japan for the first time. Sixty-four years later, in the 9/11 attack, her likeness was one of three surviving artifacts at Helen Keller International, which sustained major damage in the fire.

Acknowledgments

Grateful appreciation to the following journals which published these poems, some under slightly different titles or in different forms:

Crab Orchard Review: "Coming Through Fire," a finalist in the 2014 Richard Peterson Prize competition associated with the magazine.

Kenyon Review Online: "Encounter in Montgomery," "In Which Helen Puts to Rest the Mirror" and "The Myth of W-a-t-e-r"

The Louisville Review: "The Exquisite Instrument That Will Make an Ear" and "Memory of Ivy Green"

The New Sound: A Journal of Interdisciplinary Art and Literature: "Imaginary Farewell from Russell Cone to Helen Keller" and "First Entry, After Midnight"

PMS (PoemMemoirStory) 2010: "Silence" and "Soliloquy"

Redux: A literary journal: "This Day," "Silence," and "Soliloquy" (Note: *Redux*, an online journal, republishes poems previously in print journals but not yet in book form.)

Southern Women's Review: "This Day" and "The Little Boy Next Door"

Still: The Journal 2011 Poetry Contest, finalist: "What Helen Saw / What Helen Said"

Stone, River, Sky: An Anthology of Georgia Poets: "Enrico Caruso Remembers Helen Keller: 1918"

storySouth: "First Dream of the Tennessee"

Thirty Three: An [niversary] Anthology of Negative Capability Magazine: "With the Martha Graham Dance Company"

"This Day" and "With the Martha Graham Dance Company" were staged in *Page to Stage*, under the direction of Tina F. Turley, Theater Tuscaloosa, Shelton State Community College, April 2007. In March 2011 Turley directed a recital reading of thirteen poems from the manuscript in progress, with veteran actors from Theater Tuscaloosa.

With Gratitude

During the course of my work on this book, many people have helped with suggestions, encouragement, and the gift of space to write. For his wise council, keen eye, and his unswerving dedication to the integrity of the line, I thank Louie Skipper. I would also like to thank Anita M. Garner and Leslea Newman who read and commented on early drafts of the manuscript. Thanks to Tina Turley, Pinky Bass, Jay Lamar, Sena Jeter Naslund, and the Spalding University brief-residency MFA community for their continuing encouragement. Gratitude to John Scott who located Mildred Keller Tyson's home in Montgomery for me at a crucial early time. For the gift of sanctuary: Nana Lampton, dear friend and encourager; Skip Jones and the Board of Directors of the Fairhope Center for the Writing Arts who make a place for writers; Eleanor Inge and Stephen Baker. I am grateful to the Alabama State Council on the Arts for an Artist Fellowship in Literature which allowed me to bring the book to completion. Sincere thanks to the Council for supporting all literary arts in Alabama. I would also like to acknowledge Carl Augusto, President, and the staff of the American Foundation for the Blind (located in New York City) for hosting "Helen Keller: A Daring Adventure" in 2009 and for my visit there. To all who listened or shared impressions and guidance, I am grateful. To my mother, Katherine W. Thompson, this book is dedicated with love and appreciation for teaching me to love language and so much more.

Jeanie Thompson's poetry collections and chapbooks include *Lotus and Psalm, How to Enter the River, Litany for a Vanishing Landscape, Ascent, Witness, White for Harvest: New and Selected Poems,* and *The Seasons Bear Us.* Thompson holds the MFA from the University of Alabama, where she was founding editor of the literary journal *Black Warrior Review.* Twice awarded an Artist Fellowship in Literature from the Alabama State Council on the Arts for her poetry, Thompson is executive director of the award-winning Alabama Writers' Forum, a statewide literary arts organization in Montgomery. She teaches in the Spalding University low-residency MFA Writing Program in Louisville, Kentucky.